PROVERBS

Rose Visual
Bible Studies

D1600674

R SE
PUBLISHING

Proverbs
Rose Visual Bible Studies

©2020 Rose Publishing, LLC

Published by Rose Publishing
An imprint of Hendrickson Publishing Group

Rose Publishing, LLC
P.O. Box 3473
Peabody, Massachusetts 01961–3473 USA
www.HendricksonPublishingGroup.com

ISBN 978-162862-860-9

Author: Jessica Curiel

Scriptures taken from the Holy Bible, New International Version®, NIV®. Copyright © 1973, 1978, 1984, 2011 by Biblica, Inc.™ Used by permission of Zondervan. All rights reserved worldwide. www.zondervan.com The "NIV" and "New International Version" are trademarks registered in the United States Patent and Trademark Office by Biblica, Inc.™

Scripture quotations marked (NLT) are taken from the Holy Bible, New Living Translation, copyright ©1996, 2004, 2015 by Tyndale House Foundation. Used by permission of Tyndale House Publishers, a Division of Tyndale House Ministries, Carol Stream, Illinois 60188. All rights reserved.

Images used under license from Shutterstock.com: Paul Aniszewski, cover, p. 5; Ross Gordon Henry, p. 3, 7; Becky Starsmore, p. 3, 23; TTStudio, p. 3, 37; Anna Puzatykh, p. 3, 53; Kletr, p. 3, 65; LightField Studios, p. 3, 81; Chat Karen Studio, p. 3, 97; P.D.T.N.C., p. 8, 22; Gustavo Frazao, p. 9; Christophe Testi, p. 11; Lotus_studio, p. 14; file404, p. 16; Purple clouds, p. 2, 36; S_Photo, p. 24, 36; TACartoons, p. 25; kpboonjit, p. 27; Creatopic, p. 27; In Green, p. 29; Patrice6000, p. 32; a1 vector, p. 38, 52; Africa Studio, p. 39, 67; Fotokostic, p. 43; Krakenimages.com, p. 47; naskami, p. 54; Bk87, p. 55; Chanintorn.v, p. 58; Selma ARSLAN, p. 60; Zolnierek, p. 66, 80; eveleen, p. 72; Martial Red, p. 73 (fist); davooda, p. 73 (moneybag); JETACOM AUTOFOCUS, p. 74 (money exchange); GoodStuff, p. 74 (sword); KieferPix, p. 82, 96; dugdax, p. 83; runLenarun, p. 86; Vita Stocker, p. 87; popcic, p. 88 (crown); Aygun Ali, p. 88 (woman); Monkey Business Images, p. 89; Rasulov, p. 90; ART STOCK CREATIVE (green leaf border); P Maxwell Photography, p. 98; Amenic181, p. 101; Keep Smiling Photography, p. 103; Happy Art, icons (book, lightbulb, compass, plant).

King Solomon by Simeon Solomon (1872 or 1874), National Gallery of Art, p. 13; *Hezekiah, King of Judah* by Hippolyte Flandrin (1856–1863), Van Day Truex Fund, 1985, Metropolitan Museum of Art, p. 86.

Printed in the United States
010520VP

Contents

"The fear of the LORD is the beginning of wisdom, and knowledge of the Holy One is understanding."

Proverbs 9:10

Proverbs

King Solomon was said to have wisdom "as measureless as the sand on the seashore" (1 Kings 4:29). While much of the book of Proverbs is a collection of King Solomon's wise words, it's hardly a book just for kings. The first few verses of Proverbs chapter one tell us exactly who this book is for.

The book of Proverbs is ...

"For gaining wisdom and instruction" (v. 2).

> If want to learn how to live more wisely, then Proverbs is for you.

"For doing what is right and just and fair" (v. 3).

> If you long for justice in our world, then Proverbs is for you.

"For giving prudence to those who are simple" (v. 4).

> If you've ever felt a little naïve or unsure of what to do, then Proverbs is most certainly for you.

"Let the wise listen and add to their learning" (v. 5).

> If you're an old pro at living wisely, then Proverbs is *still* for you.

"For understanding proverbs and parables, the sayings and riddles of the wise" (v. 6).

And if you want to have a deeper knowledge of God's Word, then Proverbs is definitely for you.

You don't need to have Solomon's "measureless" wisdom to get started. You just need to begin where Proverbs says all true insight and understanding originates: *"The fear of the LORD is the beginning of knowledge"* (v. 7).

In this six-session study on the book of Proverbs, we'll journey through the major sections of the book and look closely at some of its main themes. If you want to read the entire book of Proverbs from beginning to end, follow the optional reading plan provided for each session, which is about five chapters a week.

1
WHERE
WISDOM BEGINS

Proverbs about the
Fear of the Lord

There are hundreds of wise sayings in the book of Proverbs covering all sorts of topics. There are wise words about business dealings, the courts, making money, working hard, marriage, children, parents, friends, food and drink, and what we say with our mouths and do from our hearts.

But Proverbs is not a "self-help" book. Its purpose is not to teach us how to get ahead in business, have a great spouse and kids, be admired, or make money. This might seem a bit paradoxical. That's because the book of Proverbs is not ultimately about making *good* choices (though it certainly includes that); it's about making *godly* choices. These are the kinds of choices in life that bring honor and glory to our Maker—or, as Proverbs would put it, choices that demonstrate "the fear of the LORD" (Prov. 1:7).

The fear of the Lord is not a sense of terror, but one of profound reverence. It's a deep sense of who God is and who we are in relation to him. It's a clear understanding that God is the creator, sustainer, savior, judge, and owner of the whole universe. It means trusting *his* definition of what is good and evil, right and wrong, wise and foolish. The starting point of wise living and its end goal are an all-embracing relationship with God.

Read It

Key Proverbs to Read

- ❑ Proverbs 1:1–7
- ❑ Proverbs 9:10
- ❑ Proverbs 14:27

Optional Reading Plan

- ❑ **DAY 1:** Proverbs 1
- ❑ **DAY 2:** Proverbs 2
- ❑ **DAY 3:** Proverbs 3
- ❑ **DAY 4:** Proverbs 4
- ❑ **DAY 5:** Proverbs 5

The key proverbs to read cover select Bible verses and passages on the session's topic. The optional reading plan takes you through the book of Proverbs chapter by chapter for five days each week.

"The fear of the LORD is the beginning of knowledge, but fools despise wisdom and instruction."

PROVERBS 1:7

Know It

1. What are some things Proverbs 1:1–7 says that we will gain from reading the book?

   Wisdom, instruction, understanding, doing what is right & just & fair Knowledge to the young, guidance

2. Who are the different types of characters mentioned in the first seven verses of Proverbs?

   Simple, young, wise, discerning fools

3. Read these other proverbs about the "fool" from Proverbs 1:7.

   ❏ Proverbs 1:22

   ❏ Proverbs 10:23

   ❏ Proverbs 15:5

   What characterizes the fool? (Hint: What's his attitude toward the things of God?)

What Is Wisdom?

The book of Proverbs is usually grouped with other books in the Bible called *poetic and wisdom literature*. In addition to Proverbs, these writings include the songs in the book of Psalms, the story of a wise man named Job, and the philosophical musings in Ecclesiastes.

So what's *wisdom* exactly?

Wisdom (*hokmah* in Hebrew) is often defined as the ability to make godly choices. In the Bible, wisdom is tightly connected to creation. The way God created the universe has a direct effect on the way nature and society behave. In an important sense, wisdom is the ability to see life and the world the way God sees them. Wisdom is practical knowledge that allows people to live fully.

Being wise is not only head-knowledge. In Proverbs, wisdom is not solely philosophical or theoretical; it's down-to-earth and practical. For example, a craftsman in the book of Exodus is said to be filled with wisdom (*hokmah*) to make "artistic designs" and "cut and set stones [and] to work in wood" (Ex. 31:3–5). Wisdom in Proverbs is not just about knowing what to do; it's about actually doing it. To put this in not-so-spiritual terms, a person might *know* all about the negative effects that a super-sized soda and fries might have on their health, but it's the wise person who puts that knowledge into practice and heads toward the salad bar instead!

Jesus said the wise person is one who not only hears his words, but does them: "Therefore everyone who hears these words of mine and puts them into practice is like a wise man who built his house on the rock. The rain came down, the streams rose, and the winds blew and beat against that house; yet it did not fall, because it had its foundation on the rock."

Matthew 7:24–25

Who Wrote Proverbs?

The book of Proverbs identifies several writers:

- Israel's King Solomon is the main writer (Prov. 1:1; 10:1; 25:1). The book of 1 Kings tells us that Solomon spoke three thousand proverbs during his lifetime (1 Kings 4:32).

- Some proverbs were compiled by "the men of Hezekiah king of Judah," almost three centuries after Solomon (Prov. 25:1).

- Other writers are Agur, King Lemuel, and "the wise" (Prov. 22:17; 24:23; 30:1; 31:1). Nothing more is known about them.

Wise King Solomon

The Bible says that King Solomon's wisdom was "greater than the wisdom of all the people of the East, and greater than all the wisdom of Egypt" (1 Kings 4:30).

So how did he get so wise?

Here's the story: Solomon, the young heir of the great King David, had just been crowned king of Israel when, in a dream, God made him an astounding offer: "Ask for whatever you want me to give you" (1 Kings 3:5). All he had to do was ask. Would he ask for unlimited wealth, a long life, or even more power? No, he asked for wisdom. So God gave him a "wise and discerning heart" (1 Kings 3:12). Solomon's skillful leadership, his just rulings, and his discernment in governing became known far and wide. "From all nations people came to listen to Solomon's wisdom, sent by all the kings of the world, who had heard of his wisdom" (1 Kings 4:34). Because he had chosen wisdom from the Lord instead of earthly things, the Bible tells us that God was so pleased that he granted Solomon the things he did not ask for: wealth, honor, and a long life (1 Kings 3:13–14).

King Solomon

Many centuries later, Jesus would tell his followers—who were worrying about what to eat, what to drink, what to wear, and chasing after the things of this world—to put first things first: "Seek first [God's] kingdom and his righteousness, and all these things will be given to you as well" (Matt. 6:33).

How Is the Book of Proverbs Arranged?

At first glance, the book of Proverbs may look like a mishmash of random sayings. But it's not. Though the book has over nine hundred proverbs on dozens of topics, it's actually a curated collection.

Think of surveying the book of Proverbs like walking through an art museum filled with sculptures, paintings, and engravings. Each art piece can be its own stand-alone work to be pondered and appreciated. But there are also rooms with different groupings of works—some arranged by artist, some by theme, and others by medium. There is an intentional flow from one end of the building to the other, yet you can also meander your way through the rooms in any given direction and still appreciate the collection.

The book of Proverbs has many short and memorable stand-alone sayings, but it also has carefully selected groups of sayings, a few allegorical mini-stories, poems, straight-forward teacherly instructions, and even a prayer mixed in with some odd riddles. Here is a basic outline of this curated collection, the *flow* of Proverbs:

➤ **Introduction: Who and What This Book Is For** (1:1–7)

➤ **A Father's Plea and Warnings, plus the Call of Wisdom and Folly** (1:8–9:18)

➤ **First Collection of Solomon's Proverbs** (10:1–22:16)

➤ **Thirty Sayings of the Wise** (22:17–24:22)

➤ **Further Sayings of the Wise** (24:23–34)

➤ **Second Collection of Solomon's Proverbs** (25:1–29:27)

➤ **Sayings of Agur** (30:1–33)

➤ **Sayings of King Lemuel's Mother** (31:1–9)

➤ **Poem of the Wife of Noble Character** (31:10–31)

Some Tips for Reading Proverbs

- **MEDITATE ON A SINGLE PROVERB, LIKE YOU WOULD AN ART PIECE IN A MUSEUM.**

    Ponder the proverb's meaning. Let its truth sink in and become part of your life.

    Example: "The fear of the LORD is a fountain of life, turning a person from the snares of death" (Prov. 14:27). Picture the fountain and the snares, and consider what it means for you personally to fear the Lord.

- **LOOK AT A GROUP OF PROVERBS ACCORDING TO TOPIC OR A SECTION.**

    Individual proverbs are meant to be concise and memorable, not comprehensive. A single proverb isn't designed to give you the whole picture. The proverbs teach us how to live godly lives, but are not a "one size fits all" for every circumstance. It takes wisdom to know when and how to apply a particular proverb.

    Example: Proverbs 26:4 says, "Do not answer a fool … or you will be just like him," but the very next verse says, "Answer a fool … or he will be wise in his own eyes." So which should you do? Perhaps both at different times. A wise person knows when it's best to respond and when it's best to let things be.

- **REMEMBER THAT PROVERBS ARE NOT PROMISES OR GUARANTEES.**

    You've probably heard the expression "an apple a day keeps the doctor away." But we all know that some illnesses require immediate medical attention—not an apple. It's the same with biblical proverbs. The book of Proverbs is meant to help us live godly lives, not guarantee an outcome if we follow a list of do's and don'ts.

Example: "Lazy hands make for poverty, but diligent hands bring wealth" (Prov. 10:4). Though this is generally the case, it's certainly still possible that a derelict person might win the lottery and a hard worker might lose their life savings to tragedy.

- **KNOW THAT PROVERBS WILL HELP US BETTER UNDERSTAND GOD'S HEART.**

While the book isn't a course in theological doctrines, the proverbs do show us what things the Lord loves and desires for his children, and what harmful things in the world he longs to keep us from.

Example: "The LORD disciplines those he loves, as a father the son he delights in" (Prov. 3:12).

Lost in Translation

The book of Proverbs was written in ancient Hebrew, starting as far back as the tenth century BC. Since there is usually more than one way to translate a Hebrew word or phrase into English, reading Proverbs in different Bible versions can help us pick up on the nuances that sometimes get lost in translation, especially when we come across obscure sayings and idioms. Consider how Proverbs 9:10 is translated in these three English versions:

KJV	The fear of the LORD is the beginning of wisdom: and the knowledge of the holy is understanding.
NLT	Fear of the LORD is the foundation of wisdom. Knowledge of the Holy One results in good judgment.
CEV	Respect and obey the LORD! This is the beginning of wisdom. To have understanding, you must know the Holy God.

Real Wisdom

Jesus was the wisest person to walk this earth. (Yes, even wiser than old King Solomon!) In Luke 9, Jesus tells his disciples that he would soon be laying down his own life for their sake. Then, he goes on to explain to them what it really means to *follow* him, to truly *save* one's life:

> Whoever wants to be my disciple must deny themselves and take up their cross daily and follow me. Whoever wants to save their life will lose it, but whoever loses their life for me will save it. What good is it for someone to gain the whole world, and yet lose or forfeit their very self? (Luke 9:24–25)

It's ironic, isn't it? To save one's life, one must lose it. The wisest thing to do is not to "gain the whole world;" it's to lose your life in Jesus. Real wisdom is surrendering yourself to the Lord and, in that way, gaining full and lasting life in him.

"Not until we have become humble and teachable, standing in awe of God's holiness and sovereignty, acknowledging our own littleness, distrusting our own thoughts, and willing to have our minds turned upside down, can divine wisdom become ours."

— J. I. Packer

Life Application Questions

1. Who is a wise person you know? What about them makes them wise?

2. How would you explain what it means to "fear the Lord"? What should this posture toward God look like in our lives and our churches today?

3. Can a person live wisely—following the practical advice in Proverbs—without God? Why or why not?

4. Why might someone "despise wisdom and instruction" (Prov. 1:7)? Can you think of a time when you felt like that?

5. Read Matthew 7:24–27. What are some "sands" people build their lives on? What is the "rock"? How has this principle been illustrated in your life so far?

6. What do you hope to learn from this study on the book of Proverbs? In what areas do you feel like you need some guidance, a deeper understanding, better insight, or maybe even some discipline from the Lord?

Notes

TWO
INVITATIONS

*Proverbs about
Wisdom and Folly*

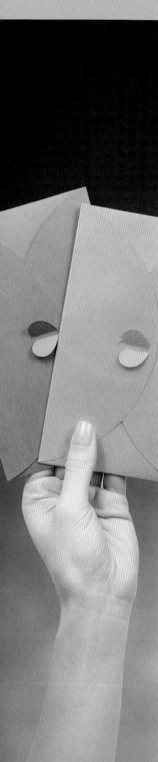

Written more than three centuries ago, *The Pilgrim's Progress* is one of the most popular Christian books of all time. Its imaginative story follows the journey of a pilgrim named Christian who travels from the City of Destruction to the Celestial City. On his way, he encounters many lively characters, like Evangelist, Mr. Worldly Wiseman, and even Giant Despair. Some of these characters help Christian onward to his destination, while others try to divert him onto dangerous paths. *The Pilgrim's Progress* is an *allegory*—a story whose characters and events represent specific ideas or qualities. Stories like this endure throughout the ages because their themes are timeless and their characters relatable. They resonate with us today, even in our fast-paced, technology-saturated world.

The book of Proverbs also has allegorical features. Like the pilgrim meeting people on his journey, we also meet some lively characters in Proverbs. There is the loving father instructing his son; the young man facing decisions between the path of wickedness and the way of godly living; and there's Lady Wisdom and Dame Folly calling out to passersby in the city streets.

In this session of our study, we'll see how God's Word in Proverbs uses vivid imagery and characters to appeal not only to our minds, but also to our imaginations.

Read It

Key Proverbs to Read

- ❏ Proverbs 3:1–18
- ❏ Proverbs 9:1–18

Optional Reading Plan

- ❏ **DAY 1:** Proverbs 6:1–19
- ❏ **DAY 2:** Proverbs 6:20–35
- ❏ **DAY 3:** Proverbs 7
- ❏ **DAY 4:** Proverbs 8
- ❏ **DAY 5:** Proverbs 9

This reading takes you to the end of the first major section of Proverbs.

"Blessed are those who find wisdom, those who gain understanding, for she is more profitable than silver and yields better returns than gold."

PROVERBS 3:13–14

Know It

1. Write down three (or more) things that the father is instructing his son to do in chapter 3. Which jump out to you as most significant, and why?

2. What do you observe about the two dinner invitations in chapter 9? How are the they similar and different? What is on the menu? Who are the guests?

3. Wisdom, Folly, the father, and the son are the main characters in these passages, but what other figures are also mentioned?

The Caricatures of Proverbs

Humorous isn't a word people often use to describe the Bible. But some of the characters we meet in Proverbs can seem rather amusing:

- Consider the sluggard who is so lazy that he won't even bother to feed himself! "A sluggard buries his hand in the dish; he is too lazy to bring it back to his mouth" (Prov. 26:15).

- Or how about the wife who has bickered her husband out of the house? "Better to live on a corner of the roof than share a house with a quarrelsome wife" (Prov. 21:9).

But then there are the characters who are no laughing matter: the fool who rejects God, the adulterer who ensnares the wayward, the glutton who ends his days in poverty, and Dame Folly who leads people to death. On the other end of the spectrum are the noble characters: the wise wife who builds her house, the son who listens the instruction of his father and mother, the righteous who are kind to the poor, and Lady Wisdom who leads people to life.

It might be helpful to think of these figures in Proverbs less as characters and more as *caricatures*. Caricatures are portraits of individuals with prominent features exaggerated. In Proverbs, the portraits of the wise and foolish are exaggerated to clearly illustrate two opposite paths for our lives—two choices, or in the imagery of Proverbs 9, two banquet invitations. In this sense, the caricatures are teaching tools used to highlight the stark differences between the ultimate ends of each path.

The characters might be exaggerated, but they're also familiar. At times, aren't we all tempted to be lazy like the sluggard or recklessly indulgent like the glutton? But at other times, we are wise like the prudent son and diligent like the woman of noble character. Or maybe we're often somewhere in the middle, like the "simple" (the naïve, the inexperienced) who struggle choosing between the paths of wisdom and foolishness. In this way, Proverbs invites us to find ourselves in the characters of the book.

What Is Folly?

Folly (*sikluth* in Hebrew) is also translated as "foolishness." In Proverbs, being a "fool" doesn't mean acting silly or being a class clown. Nor does it necessarily mean being naïve or young and inexperienced, which is characteristic of the "simple" (Prov. 1:4). Instead, foolishness refers to an obstinate heart opposed to the things of God (Prov. 13:9). The fool, Dame Folly, and the mocker in Proverbs all represent a path that leads to ruin. Wisdom, by contrast, is the path toward holiness and a heart in tune with the things of God (Prov. 3:13).

Ancient Wisdom Literature

Israel's neighboring kingdoms, like those of Mesopotamia and Egypt, had their own versions of wisdom literature. For example, some ancient Near East writings take the form of a father giving advice to a son on the cusp of adulthood. In one Egyptian text, *Instruction for Merikare* (c. 2100 BC), a pharaoh gives his son instructions for ruling effectively. The Egyptians also worshiped *Maat*, the goddess Wisdom.

Israel did not live in isolation from their surrounding cultures, so it's not surprising that their manner of writing reflected common ancient forms and styles. In fact, the Bible tells us that before settling in Canaan, the tribes of Israel spent four hundred years living in Egypt.

However, there are some important differences between these writings and the wisdom literature of Proverbs. In other wisdom texts, there is much confidence placed in one's own ability and effort to become wise. Proverbs, on the other hand, warns us not to be "wise in your own eyes," to be careful about relying "on your own understanding," and instead to "trust in the LORD with all your heart" (Prov. 3:5–7). In Proverbs, the character of Wisdom is always a personification of a concept—not a goddess to be worshiped. Another difference is that in Egyptian wisdom writings, the son being advised is almost always an elite ruler; biblical proverbs include privileged classes, but they are meant for all people. Proverbs locates the foundation—or the first and most important source—of wisdom in the fear of the Lord. This is unlike any other ancient wisdom text.

ANCIENT NEAR EAST WISDOM TEXTS	THE BOOK OF PROVERBS
Some written in a father's voice to a son, usually an elite ruler and heir.	Mostly written as a father to a son. Some parts seem to be directed to a privileged son, but the wisdom in Proverbs is meant for all social classes (Prov. 1:20–21; 9:3–4).
In Egyptian texts, Wisdom is a goddess, a deity to be worshiped.	Wisdom is personified; only God is to be worshiped (Prov. 2:6; 3:9, 19; 15:33; 22:4).
Emphasis on a person's own ability to become wise.	Fear of the Lord is where wisdom begins; trust in him and become wise (Prov. 1:7; 3:5–6; 9:10).
Practical advice about wise living, particularly ruling a society.	Practical advice about wise living, but always in obedience to the Lord and acknowledgment of his sovereignty (Prov. 5:21; 15:3; 19:21; 21:31).

Reading Proverbs Today

The book of Proverbs was written in ancient Israel and with a form and style similar to other ancient Near Eastern literature. This was an era in which kings ruled with absolute authority, the wealthy had servants and slaves, and only sons received formal education. Modern readers of Proverbs will quickly notice that much of the book is written from a perspective of fatherly advice to a youthful son. You'll find proverbial wisdom about finding a good wife (Prov. 18:22), but none about choosing a good husband; and many warnings to steer clear of the adulterous woman (Prov. 22:14), but none about avoiding the cheating man.

Though set in a particular time and place in history, the wisdom of Proverbs is meant for all people. Consider the invitation of Lady Wisdom in the first few chapters. She calls out to everyone from the city walls, in the public square, and at the city gate (Prov. 1:20–21). The gate of a city was the place where everything happened—local leaders met, court was held, and business was conducted in a bustling public marketplace. The scene pictured here is that of Wisdom inviting all people—young and old, men and women, rich and poor. As the story of Lady Wisdom's banquet in chapter 9 explains, "She calls from the highest point of the city, 'Let all who are simple come to my house!'" (Prov. 9:3–4).

A crucial part of interpreting Scripture—and especially ancient wisdom literature like Proverbs—is understanding its original setting and culture, and then applying its timeless principles to our lives today. The apostle Paul explained in the New Testament (nearly ten centuries after the earliest proverbs were written):

> "Everything that was written in the past was written to teach us, so that through the endurance taught in the Scriptures and the encouragement they provide we might have hope." (Rom. 15:4)

Our social structures, family dynamics, and cultures may change, but human nature remains surprisingly constant. We are still in need of godly wisdom—of instructions, warnings, and advice—as much as anyone ever was in ancient Israel.

"Real satisfaction comes not in understanding God's motives, but in understanding His character, in trusting in His promises, and in leaning on Him and resting in Him as the Sovereign who knows what He is doing and does all things well."

— Joni Eareckson Tada

Live It

With All Your Heart

One of the most famous passages in Proverbs is found in chapter 3:

> "Trust in the LORD with all your heart and lean not on your own understanding; in all your ways submit to him, and he will make your paths straight." (Prov. 3:5–6)

The word for *heart* is from the Hebrew word *leb*. In the Old Testament, *leb* can refer to one's physical heart (Ex. 28:29–30), but most often, the Bible depicts the heart as that immaterial part of our human personality where we feel, think, and decide.

In the book of Proverbs, the heart is where wisdom and foolishness in our lives originate. In chapter 3, the father urges the son to keep his teachings "in your heart" (verse 1); write love and faithfulness "on the tablet of your heart" (verse 3); and trust in God "with all your heart" (verse 5). No wonder we're told to "above all else, guard your heart, for everything you do flows from it" (Prov. 4:23).

Underlying the hundreds of wise instructions in the book of Proverbs is the foundation of trusting in God with all our heart. Like Dame Folly's banquet invitation that turns out to be a feast for the dead, the world is full of temptations and false promises.

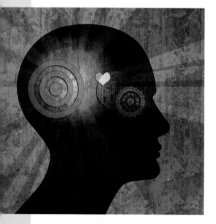

Trusting God means believing that our heavenly Father loves us and that his will for our lives is far better than the way of the world. In the New Testament, Jesus said, "Don't let your hearts be troubled. Trust in God, and trust also in me" (John 14:1 NLT). For troubled, tempted, and unsure hearts, torn between God's wise way and the world's foolish path, the key is trusting in the Lord with all that we are because of all that he is.

Life Application Questions

1. As you read the book of Proverbs, which was written in a particular era and society, what challenges do you find in interpreting and applying it today?

2. Why do we sometimes turn to folly when it leads to harm? On the flip side, why is it sometimes hard to choose wisdom when it leads to life?

3. What are some wise words your parents or other older adults have given you? At the time, did you recognize them as good advice?

4. Read Luke 2:52 and Mark 6:2 where Jesus is described as wise—*amazingly* wise. What makes Jesus unlike any other wise sage in history or religions?

5. What does it mean to trust God with all your heart? Do you see this kind of trust modeled in your home and your church?

6. When was a time in your life in which you trusted God against the competing voices in the world? When was a time you wish you *had* trusted God?

DAILY BREAD

Proverbs about
Work and Wealth

Daily Bread

Did you know that there is only one prayer in the book of Proverbs? It's tucked in near the end of the book. The writer of this section of Proverbs prays a simple prayer:

> Give me neither poverty nor riches, but give me only my daily bread. Otherwise, I may have too much and disown you and say, "Who is the LORD?" Or I may become poor and steal, and so dishonor the name of my God. (Prov. 30:8–9)

Two things mentioned in this prayer—honoring God's name and our daily bread—are echoed in the most famous prayer in the Bible, the Lord's Prayer (Matt. 6:9–13). It begins with "Our Father in heaven, hallowed be your name" and concludes with requests for our most important needs: forgiveness, deliverance from evil, and for God to "give us today our daily bread." It, too, is a simple prayer packed with meaning.

Bread in both prayers implies sustenance. It's about our heavenly Father gifting us with enough of what we need to get us through each day. As Proverbs 30 warns, we should not desire so much or so little that we end up forgetting the Lord and dishonoring his name.

In this session, we'll look at proverbs about our daily "breads"—work, money, food, and drink—and what we do with these things that the Lord has given us.

Read It

Key Proverbs to Read

- ❏ Proverbs 10:4–5
- ❏ Proverbs 11:24–26, 28
- ❏ Proverbs 12:11
- ❏ Proverbs 15:16–17
- ❏ Proverbs 21:17, 20
- ❏ Proverbs 22:7
- ❏ Proverbs 30:8–9

Optional Reading Plan

- ❏ **DAY 1:** Proverbs 10–11
- ❏ **DAY 2:** Proverbs 12
- ❏ **DAY 3:** Proverbs 13
- ❏ **DAY 4:** Proverbs 14
- ❏ **DAY 5:** Proverbs 15

This reading begins the first collection of Solomon's proverbs.

"Give me neither poverty nor riches, but give me only my daily bread."

PROVERBS 30:8

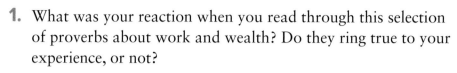

Know It

1. What was your reaction when you read through this selection of proverbs about work and wealth? Do they ring true to your experience, or not?

2. Which actions and character traits are esteemed in these proverbs? Which are discouraged?

3. Read about the different types of proverbs on the following pages. Which types do you notice from your reading of Proverbs for this session?

Types of Proverbs

Proverbs 10 begins the first collection of the individual sayings of King Solomon (Prov. 10:1–22:16). The first nine chapters about wisdom and folly are more poetic and abstract than the chapters that follow. The 375 sayings in chapters 10–22 are also about wisdom and folly, but they're more down-to-earth—practical advice about daily, godly living. In short, they're about wisdom lived out.

The word *proverb* (*masal* in Hebrew) can also be translated as "parable." Like the parables of Jesus, which are concise and practical stories that teach eternal truths, proverbs too are brief expressions of truth—though even more brief than Jesus' parables. These short, memorable sayings are the kinds of proverbs Bible readers are probably more familiar with—sayings like "The borrower is slave to the lender" (Prov. 22:7) and "Pride goes before destruction" (Prov. 16:18).

The proverbs cover a variety of topics: speech, relationships, humility, pride, anger, friendship, honesty, and (what we're focusing on in this session) work, laziness, money, and generosity. Taken together, the proverbs seek to answer a basic question: How does a wise person live?

Bible scholars categorize the numerous sayings in Proverbs in many different ways: sometimes according to their sentence structure, by theme or topic, or by the sound and rhyme of the Hebrew words. Knowing the distinctions between the types of proverbs will help you better understand the main point of each of proverb and avoid misinterpretation.

Here are four common types of proverbs found in the book (though there are certainly more).

TYPE	DESCRIPTION	EXAMPLE
Truism	These proverbs are observations about the way the world works. They invite the reader to exclaim, "How true!" These proverbs are not prescribing how the world should be, but only how it is. They help us navigate the world as it is, not how we wish it were.	"The poor are shunned even by their neighbors, but the rich have many friends" (Prov. 14:20).
This, Not That	These proverbs describe what a person should do and be like—or not do and not be like. They compare two dissimilar actions and behaviors or character traits. Basically, these proverbs are saying, "Do this, not that."	"The LORD detests dishonest scales, but accurate weights find favor with him" (Prov. 11:1).
Better Than	These proverbs call us to focus on what matters most by comparing two scenarios. Both scenes might not be ideal, but one is certainly *better than* the other.	"Better a dry crust with peace and quiet than a house full of feasting, with strife" (Prov. 17:1).
Word Pictures	These proverbs paint vivid word pictures through metaphors and similes. Their imaginative descriptions drive home the point about how good or how bad something can be.	"Food gained by fraud tastes sweet, but one ends up with a mouth full of gravel" (Prov. 20:17).

Parallelism in Proverbs

Parallelism is an important feature of biblical proverbs. English proverbs normally have one line:

> A penny saved is a penny earned.

Hebrew proverbs usually have two:

> A fool finds pleasure in wicked schemes,
> but a person of understanding delights in wisdom.
> (PROV. 10:23)

Parallelism means that the second line of the verse advances the thought of the first line. Determining how this movement occurs allows us to understand the sense and meaning of the proverb. Sometimes the second line repeats or reinforces the point of the first line. This is called *synonymous parallelism:*

> From the fruit of their lips people are filled with good things,
> and the work of their hands brings them reward.
> (PROV. 12:14)

Other times, the second line presents a contrast to the first. This is called *antithetical parallelism:*

> Those who work their land will have abundant food,
> but those who chase fantasies have no sense.
> (PROV. 12:11)

Finding Balance

"Work-life balance" is a buzzword these days. How do we juggle office hours and the kids' soccer practice? How do we meet schoolwork due dates and yet find "me time" (another buzzword)? The ancient Israelites were way ahead of this trend! It won't take long reading through the sayings of Proverbs to notice all the warnings about indulging in the extremes. Though Proverbs won't offer us tips for making it to class on time or paying our bills, it is full of timeless principles for a balanced perspective of work, money, food, and other provisions.

When reading through the book of Proverbs, be sure to read the proverbial sayings not only individually, but also together as a whole. Consider these disparate proverbs and the kind of picture they paint when seen together.

PROVERBS SAYS TO	... but ...	PROVERBS ALSO SAYS
Store up choice food and olive oil (21:20)	... but ...	don't hoard your grain (11:26).
Gather crops in the summer with diligent hands (10:4)	... but ...	don't wear yourself out to get rich (23:4).
Work your land to have abundant food (12:11)	... but ...	don't gorge yourself on meat and wine (23:20–21).
Gather money little by little (13:11)	... but ...	give to others without sparing (21:26).
Know that wealth is a blessing from the Lord (10:22)	... but ...	realize that wealth can make you disown the Lord (30:9).
Store your provisions in summer to plan for winter (6:8)	... but ...	remember it is the Lord who establishes your steps (16:9).

What other examples can you find in Proverbs? Write them here:

PROVERBS SAYS TO	... *but* ...	PROVERBS ALSO SAYS
	... *but* ...	
	... *but* ...	
	... *but* ...	

**"So whether you eat or drink
or whatever you do, do it all
for the glory of God."**

1 Corinthians 10:31

Reading Proverbs in Context

A superficial reading of the book of Proverbs could suggest that the world functions perfectly with what theologians call *retribution theology*: good things happen to good people and bad things happen to bad people. After all, doesn't Proverbs say, "The wages of the righteous is life, but the earnings of the wicked are sin and death" (Prov. 10:16)?

Although we can read each proverb separately, biblical proverbs were placed by divine will in a specific context. The book of Proverbs is part of a larger conversation with the other wisdom books in the Bible. Proverbs, Job, and Ecclesiastes balance and complement each other's views about wisdom, God, creation, humanity, and every important topic of the Bible.

Consider the story in the book of Job, where a "blameless and upright" man named Job loses nearly everything he has (Job 1:1). Job's three friends argue that Job must've done something sinful because God rewards the righteous and punishes the wicked. Job, however, continues to defend his own innocence. As readers, we know from the introduction in chapters one and two that Job is a righteous man who is being used and abused by Satan, with God's authorization. Job pleads for an audience with the Creator. When he finally gets one, Job does not receive answers but a series of questions. God shows that he alone is wise. Job humbly recognizes the limits of his own wisdom and declares, "Surely I spoke of things I did not understand, things too wonderful for me to know" (Job 42:3). At the end of the story, God justifies and restores Job. He also rebukes Job's friends for their foolishness.

Job's friends could be described as being "wise in [their] own eyes" (Prov. 3:7). They assumed they knew all that was going on, when they (like Job too) didn't have the full picture. We might read a proverb like, "Lazy hands make for poverty, but diligent hands bring wealth" (Prov. 10:4), and assume the reverse must also be true: a poor person *must* be lazy and a wealthy person *must* be a hard worker. But proverbs describe general principles and ultimate ends of wise and foolish ways of living. They are not "one size fits all" statements. Consider that even Proverbs says, "Better the poor whose walk is blameless than the rich whose ways are perverse" (Prov. 28:6). Riches don't necessarily indicate righteousness, and poverty doesn't mean laziness.

We should read Proverbs in light of the rest of Scripture, which calls us to recognize the limits of our own wisdom—when we think we've got the whole picture figured out—or else we'll end up like Job's foolish friends. Just as the book of Proverbs is an invitation to fall in love with Lady Wisdom, the book of Job is a reminder that we should not fall in love with our own ideas.

Money Matters

We all have different perspectives about finances based on personal experience and how we were raised. Look at the diagram below and mark on each line how you most often view money and possessions. Remember, there aren't necessarily right or wrong answers. This exercise is simply for you to take inventory of your general attitudes and assumptions.

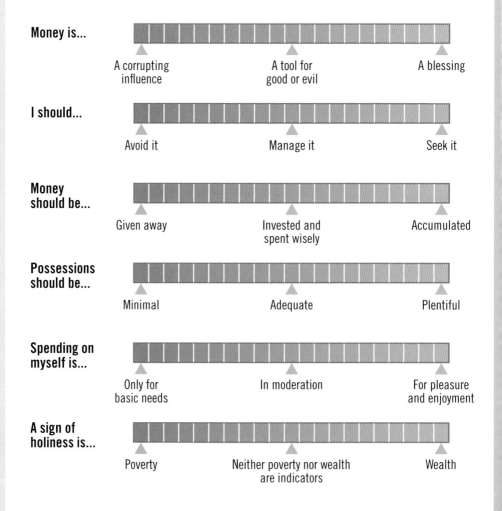

Money is...
A corrupting influence | A tool for good or evil | A blessing

I should...
Avoid it | Manage it | Seek it

Money should be...
Given away | Invested and spent wisely | Accumulated

Possessions should be...
Minimal | Adequate | Plentiful

Spending on myself is...
Only for basic needs | In moderation | For pleasure and enjoyment

A sign of holiness is...
Poverty | Neither poverty nor wealth are indicators | Wealth

Life Application Questions

1. Look at your answers on the diagram from the previous page. Whatever our feelings are about money and possessions, they need to be evaluated in light of what the Bible says. Which of your assumptions or attitudes toward finances needs to change?

2. Proverbs reminds us not to trust in riches (Prov. 11:28). Besides our bank accounts and wallets, what other types of *riches* do people trust in?

3. Overindulgence—or *gluttony*, to use a Proverbs term—harms not only our own lives, but those of the people closest to us. How have you seen overindulgences—such as in food, drink, medicines, money, gambling, spending, etc.—impact the lives of loved ones?

4. The prophet Jeremiah laments to the Lord, "Why does the way of the wicked prosper? Why do all the faithless live at ease?" (Jer. 12:1). Have you ever felt like Jeremiah when you see prosperity come to those whom you think don't deserve it? How would you answer Jeremiah's questions? How does the Bible answer these questions?

5. In ancient Israel, work usually meant manual labor, often outdoors, and it was especially important during the harvest season. What does *work* mean in your life now? How do you honor God's name in your work?

6. What are some of the kinds of *daily breads* that you ask God for? How has he provided them?

WORDS LIKE SWORDS & HONEY

Proverbs about What We Say

Words Like Swords and Honey

Those closest to us have the inside track to our hearts. The bonds we form with our loved ones by going through life's ups and downs together are priceless. It's no wonder that the things we say to each other can be words that bring the most healing when we face difficult times, but can also do the most damage when the words are thoughtless or malicious. As the book of Proverbs so vividly puts it, "gracious words are like a honeycomb, sweet to the soul and healing to the bones" (Prov. 16:24), but reckless words "pierce like swords" (Prov. 12:18).

Proverbs is a book about relationships: our relationship with our Creator, with family members, with friends, neighbors, and society in general. Our words can make those relationships better or break them. Proverbs has both encouragement and warning about what we say to one another. In this session, we'll look at how our words have "the power of life and death" (Prov. 18:21).

Read It

Key Proverbs to Read

❏ Proverbs 12:16–19

❏ Proverbs 15:18, 23

❏ Proverbs 16:23–24, 28

❏ Proverbs 17:9, 19

❏ Proverbs 18:21

❏ Proverbs 26:17–25

❏ Proverbs 27:5–6, 17

Optional Reading Plan

❏ Day 1: Proverbs 16

❏ Day 2: Proverbs 17

❏ Day 3: Proverbs 18

❏ Day 4: Proverbs 19–20

❏ Day 5: Proverbs 21:1–22:16

This reading brings you to the end of the first collection of Solomon's proverbs.

"Gracious words are a honeycomb, sweet to the soul and healing to the bones."

PROVERBS 16:24

1. What are some characteristics of quarreling in Proverbs 15:18; 17:19; 26:17?

2. What does an "apt reply" or "timely word" look like (Prov. 15:23)? What might be some examples?

3. In addition to honeycombs and swords, what other imagery from this selection of proverbs is used to describe the good and bad of speech and relationships?

Explore It

James and Proverbs

Though the letter of James was written about seven or more centuries after Proverbs, it's long been noted how these two books of the Bible resemble each other. Some scholars have even called the epistle of James the wisdom literature of the New Testament. Both books address practical matters for godly living, such as anger, humility, favoritism, our words, helping the needy, gaining wisdom, and more. The tone of both books is instructional and matter-of-fact. Consider these parallels between James and Proverbs:

INSTRUCTION	JAMES	PROVERBS
Patience	"Everyone should be quick to listen, slow to speak and slow to become angry" (James 1:19).	"Whoever is patient has great understanding, but one who is quick-tempered displays folly" (Prov. 14:29).
Careful with words	"Those who consider themselves religious and yet do not keep a tight rein on their tongues deceive themselves" (James 1:26).	"Those who guard their lips preserve their lives, but those who speak rashly will come to ruin" (Prov. 13:3).
Bragging	"The tongue is a small part of the body, but it makes great boasts. Consider what a great forest is set on fire by a small spark" (James 3:5).	"A fool's mouth lashes out with pride, but the lips of the wise protect them" (Prov. 14:3).

INSTRUCTION	JAMES	PROVERBS
Bad-mouthing	"With the tongue we praise our Lord and Father, and with it we curse human beings, who have been made in God's likeness.... This should not be" (James 3:9–10).	"Whoever derides their neighbor has no sense, but the one who has understanding holds their tongue" (Prov. 11:12).
Quarreling	"What causes fights and quarrels among you? Don't they come from your desires that battle within you?" (James 4:1).	"Whoever loves a quarrel loves sin; whoever builds a high gate invites destruction" (Prov. 17:19).

If you have the time, read the letter of James this week. It's not long; only five chapters. As you read, you'll discover even more parallels.

Speech that Builds Up and Tears Down

In the New Testament, Paul gives this important instruction: "Do not let any unwholesome talk come out of your mouths, but only what is helpful for building others up according to their needs" (Eph. 4:29). The book of Proverbs has many examples of the kinds of words that build others up and the kinds that tear others down.

 Words that Build Up

- Wise and faithful instruction (Prov. 31:26)
- Nourishing lips (Prov. 10:21)
- Honest and truthful talk (Prov. 12:19; 16:13; 24:26)
- Healing speech (Prov. 12:18)
- Kind words (Prov. 12:25)
- Knowledgeable speech (Prov. 15:7; 20:15)
- Gentle answers (Prov. 15:1; 25:15)
- A soothing tongue (Prov. 15:4)
- Aptly-spoken or well-timed words (Prov. 15:23)
- Gracious words (Prov. 15:26; 16:21, 24)
- Sharing good news (Prov. 15:30)
- Restrained speech (Prov. 17:27)

 Words that Tear Down

- Violent talk (Prov. 10:6)
- Lying (Prov. 10:18; 12:19)
- Gossiping (Prov. 11:13; 16:28; 18:8; 20:19)
- Deceitful and foolish advice (Prov. 12:5; 14:7)
- Piercing, hurtful words (Prov. 12:18)
- Rash speech (Prov. 13:3)
- Boasting and proud talk (Prov. 14:3; 27:2)
- Harsh words (Prov. 15:1)
- Quarreling (Prov. 17:14, 19; 20:3)
- Perverse talk (Prov. 19:1)
- Mocking and insulting (Prov. 22:10)
- Exaggeration (Prov. 22:13; 26:13)
- Disingenuous speech and flattery (Prov. 26:24; 29:5)

Sharpening One Another

One of the most well-known proverbs is found in chapter 27: "As iron sharpens iron, so one person sharpens another" (Prov. 27:17). A very literal translation of the second line would read, "one man sharpens another's face." In the ancient world, *face* (*panim* in Hebrew) could also refer to the edge of an ax or sword. Figuratively, the face of someone meant their whole person—their

emotions and orientation toward the world and others. In the Bible, when it's said that God hides his face that means rejection (Ps. 13:1) and when he shines his face upon someone that means favor and grace (Num. 6:25).

The image pictured in Proverbs 27:17 is that of iron tools sharpening one another, a process which makes both of them (their "faces") more effective and useful. So too, good friends improve one another by their interactions. In this proverb's metaphor—unlike some others (Prov. 5:4; 25:18)—sharpness is a good quality.

A few verses earlier in this same chapter, we're told that open rebuke is better than hidden love and that "wounds from a friend can be trusted" (Prov. 27:5–6). Sometimes the words of a good friend can feel as sharp and as hard as iron, but when they're words that need to be said and they're given from a place of love and concern, they can make the friendship stronger and both friends become more effective.

Live It

Here's an idea to help rein in a reckless tongue and to send forth healing words. Before you speak, text, post, or hit that send button, ask yourself these three simple questions:

1. IS IT TRUE?

"A truthful witness saves lives, but a false witness is deceitful" (Prov. 14:25).

2. IS IT HELPFUL?

"Anxiety weighs down the heart, but a kind word cheers it up" (Prov. 12:25).

3. IS IT NEEDED?

"Sin is not ended by multiplying words, but the prudent hold their tongues" (Prov. 10:19).

> **"Kind words can be short and easy to speak, but their echoes are truly endless."**
>
> —Mother Teresa

Life Application Questions

1. Our words travel faster and farther than they did in Bible times. With social media, smartphones, videos, and so many more ways of communicating, how should we apply the proverbs about our "tongue" to our fast-paced world today?

2. Is there a difference between arguing and quarreling? How can individuals disagree without quarreling, as Proverbs warns against?

3. Proverbs 15:18 says that a "hot-tempered person stirs up conflict." Think of a situation in which a person's quick temper and reckless words caused strife within a family, a church, or among friends. What are some helpful ways to handle similar situations in the future?

4. Do you have a hair-trigger temper yourself? What habits can help you become better at being "quick to listen, slow to speak and slow to become angry" (James 1:19)?

5. Proverbs says to have honest lips that speak the truth (Prov. 12:17) and also to "cover an offense" in love and "drop the matter" (Prov 17:9, 14). Is it possible to do both? How?

6. With whom in your life do you need to be more intentional in speaking words that build up rather than tear down? What gracious words do they need to hear from you? Make it a point to pray for them this week. Use your words in prayer to lift them up.

BETTER THAN SACRIFICE

Proverbs about Justice

Better Than Sacrifice

In Jesus' day, the Pharisees were the best law-followers around—or so they thought. They meticulously gave the religious requirement of a tenth (a tithe) of even the smallest things. This, however, didn't impress Jesus at all:

> Woe to you, teachers of the law and Pharisees, you hypocrites! You give a tenth of your spices—mint, dill and cumin. But you have neglected the more important matters of the law—justice, mercy and faithfulness. (Matt. 23:23)

In Bible times, the people of God made sacrifices at the temple to atone for sins. But no temple sacrifice, no tithe, and no religious law-following could make up for the absence of what was most important—justice, mercy, and faithfulness. As Proverbs states, "To do what is right and just is more acceptable to the Lord than sacrifice" (Prov. 21:3).

True, godly wisdom—as the introduction to Proverbs reminds us—involves "doing what is right and just and fair" (Prov. 1:3). The wise person in Proverbs is one whose actions consider the good of others, particularly those in society who are most vulnerable.

In this session, we'll look at what Proverbs says about topics such as honesty, false testimony, bribery, the courts, revenge, mercy, privilege, and power. In short, we'll see what God's Word says about *justice*.

Read It

Key Proverbs to Read

- [ ] Proverbs 17:23
- [ ] Proverbs 19:5
- [ ] Proverbs 20:23
- [ ] Proverbs 21:3

- [ ] Proverbs 22:22–23
- [ ] Proverbs 23:10–11
- [ ] Proverbs 24:11–12, 23–25, 28–29

Optional Reading Plan

- [ ] **DAY 1:** Proverbs 22:17–29
- [ ] **DAY 2:** Proverbs 23
- [ ] **DAY 3:** Proverbs 24:1–22
- [ ] **DAY 4:** Proverbs 24:23–34
- [ ] **DAY 5:** Proverbs 25–26

This reading takes you through the sayings of the wise and into the second collection of Solomon's proverbs.

"To do what is right and just is more acceptable to the LORD than sacrifice."

PROVERBS 21:3

Know It

1. According to these proverbs, what are the consequences of not acting justly toward others?

2. Look again at Proverbs 23:10–11 and 24:11–12. What is God's response to injustices?

3. Proverbs 20:23 says that dishonest scales do not please the Lord. What are some modern-day examples of "dishonest scales"?

Thirty Sayings of the Wise

Partway through Proverbs 22, a new section begins—the "sayings of the wise." No clues are given about who these wise people might have been. Nonetheless, their sayings are collected in Proverbs 22:17–24:22. They are written as admonitions from a father to his son, similar to the first nine chapters of Proverbs. These proverbs are a series of do's and (a lot more) do not's. Most Bible scholars see this section as consisting of thirty sayings (Prov. 22:20). Though there are different ways of dividing the sayings, most totals are in the ballpark of thirty—or possibly forty if the additional sayings in Proverbs 24:23–34 are also included.

The father in this section is the voice of wisdom. The son—though probably not a specific, historical person—is portrayed as a prince or an official, or at least someone in the company of society's elite. The son seems to be in a position where he could exploit the poor in court (Prov. 22:22–23), seize the property of the powerless (Prov. 22:28), dine with wealthy rulers and officials (Prov. 23:1; 24:21), and join in with those who have an abundance of wine and meats (Prov. 23:20). In other words, he is a young, privileged man who might easily think he could get away with anything. That's what makes the father's voice so important.

Again and again, the father warns the son to do what is just and right toward others, because there is a Judge higher than any human court; an all-powerful Defender of the powerless; and One who knows what is in our hearts and will mete out justice accordingly. It's a strong reminder that whatever injustices done on earth are not unseen or ignored by the Lord in heaven.

Thirty Sayings of the Wise

	INSTRUCTION	PROVERBS
1	Listen to wisdom.	22:17–21
2	Do not exploit the poor.	22:22–23
3	Do not make friends with a hot-tempered person.	22:24–25
4	Do not pledge or put up security for debts.	22:26–27
5	Do not move ancient boundary stones.	22:28
6	Be skilled in your work.	22:29
7	Do not give in to gluttony.	23:1–3
8	Do not wear yourself out to get rich.	23:4–5
9	Do not be deceived by a stingy person.	23:6–8
10	Do not speak to fools.	23:9
11	Do not seize the fields of the fatherless.	23:10–11
12	Apply your heart to instruction.	23:12
13	Do not withhold discipline from a child.	23:13–14
14	Have a wise heart and bring joy to others.	23:15–16
15	Do not envy sinners; rather, fear the Lord.	23:17–18
16	Do not drink to drunkenness or eat to gluttony.	23:19–21
17	Buy truth and keep it.	23:22–25
18	Watch out for an adulterous woman.	23:26–28
19	Do not be seduced by wine.	23:29–35
20	Do not envy the wicked and violent.	24:1–2
21	Wisdom builds a house and fills it.	24:3–4
22	Victory comes through strength and guidance.	24:5–6
23	Wisdom is too high for fools.	24:7

	INSTRUCTION	PROVERBS
24	Evil schemes destroy a reputation.	24:8–9
25	Rescue those who are being oppressed.	24:10–12
26	Finding wisdom gives future hope.	24:13–14
27	Do not steal from the righteous.	24:15–16
28	Do not gloat when your enemy falls.	24:17–18
29	Do not fret because of evildoers.	24:19–20
30	Fear the Lord and the king.	24:21–22

Thirty Teachings of Amenemope

The Teachings of Amenemope is an ancient Egyptian text dating to around 1250 BC. In this text, Amenemope instructs his young son in proper conduct. The collection of these teachings is arranged into thirty chapters. Scholars have noted how the topics of Amenemope and the Sayings of the Wise in Proverbs are strikingly similar: illegally taking territory, exploiting the poor, and being gluttonous at a dining table. Though there are similarities in topic and structure, there is no indication that Proverbs was derived from this text. These kinds of issues would have been relevant to any ruler in the ancient world, and the writers of Proverbs wrote in a style and form like other ancient Near Eastern writers (see Session 2 in this study). But one thing Proverbs does differently than other texts is to always remind the reader to "fear the LORD," knowing that he is the Judge who will make a final ruling on all the just and unjust deeds of mankind (Prov. 22:23; 24:21).

Justice, Proverbs, and the Law

The word *justice* (*mishpat* in Hebrew) occurs more than two hundred times in the Old Testament. At the heart of this word is the idea of fairness. Human nature is inclined to long for a world that is fair. We want to see bad deeds punished and good deeds rewarded. (Though admittedly, it's usually easier to want to see other people bear the consequences of their wrongs than to accept our own.) Justice, in the biblical sense, is not only about judgment of sins; it's also about restoring the harmed and freeing the oppressed. The idea of justice permeates Old Testament law and it's echoed in the book of Proverbs. Let's consider four specific topics in Proverbs all related to justice.

Testimony

The ninth commandment forbids giving false testimony (Ex. 20:16). A witness in the ancient world was even more important than in today's courts. This was a time long before forensic science, fingerprinting, DNA analysis, surveillance cameras, and the like. According to Old Testament law, a person could be convicted on the word of two witnesses (Deut. 19:15). It's no wonder that giving false testimony was considered especially heinous in ancient Israel. In fact, if a witness was found to be lying against an accused, that person would receive the same punishment as the accused would have received (Deut. 19:18–19).

In the context of ancient courts, the "lying tongue" that Proverbs warns against could be extremely harmful (Prov. 6:17). Words are powerful, and so Proverbs warns, "A false witness will not go unpunished" (Prov. 19:5). But Proverbs also encourages, "A truthful witness saves lives" (Prov. 14:25). These are the two sides of justice: both to refrain from accusing someone falsely and to actively speak up with truthful words to save lives.

Power

When Moses appointed judges among the tribes of Israel, he urged them to use their power (which was a lot in the ancient world) without bias: "Hear the disputes between your people and judge fairly, whether the case is between two Israelites or between an Israelite and a foreigner residing among you. Do not show partiality in judging" (Deut. 1:16–17). Just after God gave Moses the Ten Commandments, he also gave this instruction: "Do not deny justice to your poor people in their lawsuits. Have nothing to do with a false charge and do not put an innocent or honest person to death, for I will not acquit the guilty" (Ex. 23:6–7).

We hear a similar command in Proverbs 22:22, which says, "Do not exploit the poor because they are poor and do not crush the needy in court." A more literal translation of "in court" would be "at the gates." The city gate was the place court was held and legal transactions took place, including property rights and business deals. The *poor* or *needy* in this sense would be those who are in a weaker position. They are poor in relation to the person who has more power, money, and influence.

Bribery

In Exodus 23:8, the Lord gives a law that sounds a lot like what we find in Proverbs: "Do not accept a bribe, for a bribe blinds those who see and twists the words of the innocent."

Here is a quick survey of what Proverbs says about bribery:

- "The greedy bring ruin to their households, but the one who hates bribes will live" (Prov. 15:27).

- "A bribe is seen as a charm by the one who gives it; they think success will come at every turn" (Prov. 17:8).

- "The wicked accept bribes in secret to pervert the course of justice" (Prov. 17:23).

- "By justice a king gives a country stability, but those who are greedy for bribes tear it down" (Prov. 29:4).

A *bribe* (*shohad* in Hebrew) comes from a verb meaning "to give a gift." But a bribe, of course, is not truly a gift; it's a "gift" with strings attached. It's an inducement to get someone to do something that they otherwise wouldn't. While bribes may work like a "charm" sometimes, Proverbs warns in the strongest terms that in the end bribes will tear down a household and a country.

Revenge

One of the most all-encompassing laws of the Old Testament—and repeated by Jesus in the New Testament (Matt. 22:39)—is "Love your neighbor as yourself" (Lev. 19:18). This command in Leviticus is prefaced by another command: "Do not seek revenge or bear a grudge against anyone among your people" (Lev. 19:18).

Biblical justice is not the same as revenge. Justice is not "getting back" at someone or exchanging harm for harm and wrong for wrong. Proverbs explicitly tells us, "Do not say, 'I'll do to them as they have done to me; I'll pay them back for what they did'" (Prov. 24:29). It takes wisdom to know when an action in response to a wrong is justice, and not revenge.

Exodus 23:1–9, a passage that's all about justice, paints a practical, farm-like picture of what it means not to be revengeful: "If you come across your enemy's ox or donkey wandering off, be sure to return it. If you see the donkey of someone who hates you fallen down under its load, do not leave it there; be sure you help them with it" (Ex. 23:4–5). This is similar to Proverbs, which says, "If your enemy is hungry, give him food to eat; if he is thirsty, give him water to drink" (Prov. 25:21). This is the opposite of a revengeful, begrudging attitude that does to one's enemy as they think that person would do to them.

Proverbs tells us not to seek our own revenge, but to "wait for the LORD and he will avenge you" (Prov. 20:22). Instead of trading one injustice for another injustice, we are called to leave it in the hands of the Judge in heaven who will, in his timing, bring justice to all matters.

A Life of Justice

Jesus modeled a life of justice. He healed the wounded, treated the outcasts with compassion and the sinners with mercy, and defended the poor from the powerful. Then, at the end of his earthly ministry, he willingly suffered an injustice on our behalf. He was betrayed by one of his disciples for a bribe of thirty pieces of silver, accused by false witnesses in illegal nighttime trials, and then crucified like a criminal by the powerful Roman authorities. Yet he did not seek revenge. Instead, from the cross, he asked his heavenly Father to forgive his persecutors. His sacrificial death on the cross brought mercy and forgiveness to us. His resurrection three days later proved that death, sin, and all the injustices in the world will one day ultimately be defeated.

Fear and Trust

In the book of Deuteronomy, Moses reminds Israel's judges of what he told them when they were first appointed: "Do not show partiality in judging; hear both small and great alike. Do not be afraid of anyone, for judgment belongs to God" (Deut. 1:17). Notice how he says, "Do not be afraid of anyone." This is what Proverbs calls the fear of man: "Fear of man will prove to be a snare" (Prov. 29:25).

We might not set out to do something unjust toward another. We don't intend to use our power or influence to exploit someone. But the fear of others can push us toward doing things we might not have ever imagined we would. We fear what others might think about us or do to us, so we say something we know isn't true. We are tempted to do wrong to someone else because we're afraid that wrong will be done to us. This is when we need to be reminded of the Lord's command: "Do not follow the crowd in doing wrong … do not pervert justice by siding with the crowd" (Ex. 23:2); and also of his promise: "Whoever trusts in the LORD is kept safe" (Prov. 29:25). Instead of fearing others, we can place our trust in the One who is Judge of all.

> ## "Many seek an audience with a ruler, but it is from the LORD that one gets justice."
>
> Proverbs 29:26

Life Application Questions

1. What is a bribe and how is it different from a gift or a payment? Why do you think God's Word speaks so harshly against giving and receiving bribes?

2. What kinds of "sacrifices" do people today make that they think will excuse them (or atone) for continuing in acts of injustice?

3. Honesty isn't limited only to when we raise our right hand in court. Consider how honesty should play a role in things like insurance claims, employment contracts, selling or buying property, and filing taxes. What "fears of man" do you have that tempt you toward anything less than honesty?

4. What is the difference between justice and revenge? How can you know when something is more about seeking revenge than desiring justice?

5. Read Proverbs 24:11–12. What are some examples you see in today's world of "rescuing those being led away to death" and "holding back those staggering toward slaughter"?

6. Think about what your privileges, powers, and influences—big or small—might be. How can you use them to bring justice into your part of the world where God has placed you?

Notes

ORDINARY HEROES

Proverbs about
Character

Ordinary Heroes

Our heroes sometimes let us down: a famous athlete is found out to be doping, a big celebrity is caught on tape in a racist rant, or a beloved Christian preacher is discovered embezzling funds. No one likes to know that their favorite actor from the movies is anything but a role model in real life.

So what makes a *real* hero? Not the carefully crafted celebrity on the big screen, but a person you know who lives faithfully and who genuinely "walks the talk;" a person whose life might seem so ordinary to others, but you know that it's really quite extraordinary. They are, as the book of Proverbs says, people of "noble character" (Prov. 31:10). They do ordinary things in extraordinary ways because their actions honor God and bless those around them. Proverbs tells us to find these people, walk with them, and learn from them. They inspire us to be ordinary heroes too.

In this final session of our study, we'll look at what God's Word says about character as we wrap up the book of Proverbs with a poem about a figure of godly wisdom lived out.

Read It

Key Proverbs to Read

- ❏ Proverbs 10:9
- ❏ Proverbs 11:3, 16–17
- ❏ Proverbs 31:10–31

Optional Reading Plan

- ❏ **DAY 1:** Proverbs 27
- ❏ **DAY 2:** Proverbs 28
- ❏ **DAY 3:** Proverbs 29
- ❏ **DAY 4:** Proverbs 30
- ❏ **DAY 5:** Proverbs 31

This reading takes you through the second collection of Solomon's proverbs, the musings of Agur, the teachings of Lemuel's mother, and the poem of the wife of noble character.

"Whoever walks in integrity walks securely, but whoever takes crooked paths will be found out."

PROVERBS 10:9

Know It

1. Read Proverbs 11:3, 16 in at least three Bible translations. How are the terms *integrity*, *upright*, and *kindhearted* expressed differently? Reading in more than one translation can reveal nuances and a bigger picture of what the words mean. (You can compare Bible translations at websites like biblegateway.com and biblehub.com.)

2. The actions and traits of the woman of noble character reflect other teachings in Proverbs. What parallels from Proverbs 31 can you find for the following proverbs? (The first two in the chart are done for you.)

PROVERBS	PROVERBS 31:10–31
"Diligent hands bring wealth" (10:4).	She works vigorously (verse 17).
"Whoever is kind to the needy honors God" (14:31).	She opens her arms to the poor (verse 20).
"The wise woman builds her house" (14:1).	
"Whoever listens to [wisdom] will live in safety" (1:33).	
"A wife of noble character is her husband's crown" (12:4).	
"Wisdom is found on the lips of the discerning" (10:13).	
"Let someone else praise you, and not your own mouth" (27:2).	
"Fear of the Lord is the beginning of knowledge" (1:7).	

Explore It

The Final Chapters of Proverbs

The last few chapters of the book of Proverbs contain the second set of King Solomon's proverbs, some interesting (if at times confusing) reflections from Agur, the wise sayings from King Lemuel (or more properly, his mother's sayings), and, to endcap the book, a celebratory poem about a wife of noble character. Let's do a quick survey through each section.

Second Collection of Solomon's Proverbs
Proverbs 25:1–29:27

Like the first collection of Solomon's proverbs (Prov. 10:1–22:16), this section (chapters 25–29) consists of pithy, wise sayings from King Solomon. Proverbs 25:1 informs readers that these proverbs were "compiled by the men of Hezekiah king of Judah." Hezekiah was one of the good kings of Judah who reigned near the end of the seventh century BC—that's about three hundred years after Solomon. (Hezekiah's story can be found in 2 Kings 18–20.) The "men of Hezekiah" were presumably court scribes who copied and arranged this section (or possibly even the whole book) of Proverbs.

King Hezekiah

Musings of Agur
Proverbs 30:1–33

The words of Agur are one of three poems that round out the book of Proverbs:

- Agur (Prov. 30:1–33)

- Lemuel (Prov. 31:1–9)

- Wife of Noble Character (Prov. 31:10–31)

Agur's identity is anyone's guess. The name does not appear elsewhere in the Bible. He is only called the "son of Jakeh," though we don't know who Jakeh is either (Prov. 30:1). Agur's sayings are described as a *massa*, Hebrew for "oracle," or as some Bible translations put it, *oration, prophecy,* or *inspired utterance.* When used as a proper noun, *Massa* can refer to a tribe in northern Arabia, leading some to think that Agur may have been a wise man from Arabia, though this is far from certain.

Agur's writings are musings and observations about the world. They're more philosophical and reflective than other parts of Proverbs. They sound a lot like what we find in the books of Ecclesiastes and Job. Agur poetically reflects on human limitations and frailty ("Surely I am a brute, not a man;" Prov. 30:2) and God's transcendence ("Who has established all the ends of the earth?" Prov. 30:4). This section also includes the only prayer in the book of Proverbs (Prov. 30:7–9).

If you're reading Agur's sayings and they sound strange and hard to understand, keep in mind that it's Hebrew poetry, and like most poems, the meaning is not intended to be quickly deciphered. Poetry is meant to be meditated upon and to instill in us a sense of awe about ourselves, the world, and the God who created such complex and marvelous things.

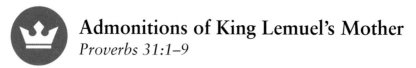

Admonitions of King Lemuel's Mother
Proverbs 31:1–9

Lemuel's name means "belonging to God." This is the only mention of King Lemuel in the Bible. Most scholars conclude that Lemuel was a non-Israelite king; he is not listed among the kings of Israel or Judah. Some think he might have been from northern Arabia because, like Agur, he gives a *massa* (Prov. 31:1).

Though these proverbs are introduced as the sayings of King Lemuel, they're the wisdom his mother taught him (Prov. 31:1). They are presented in a mother's voice to her son, much as other parts of Proverbs are as a father speaking. This section consists of a short series of admonitions to a young prince.

Poem of the Wife of Noble Character
Proverbs 31:10–31

This poem concludes the book of Proverbs. The character of this poem has been called the woman of valor, the Proverbs 31 woman, or as some older English translations put it, the valiant woman. These twenty-two verses form an acrostic poem in which each verse begins with a successive letter of the Hebrew alphabet. This structure is not unique in the Bible. For example, acrostic poems can be found in Psalms 9, 10, 112, and Lamentations 1–4.

In a way, this poem in chapter 31 is a summary of all the wisdom from the first thirty chapters. The woman pictured here fears the Lord, which, after all, is where true wisdom begins (Prov. 1:7; 31:30). She is a portrait of wisdom—the book of Proverbs lived out. Some have suggested that she is Lady Wisdom from the first nine chapters in a concrete, down-to-earth form. The teachings found in Proverbs 31 are not limited to women anymore than the father-to-son portions of Proverbs are limited to men.

This poem also has some characteristics found in ancient hymns written for military victors. In these hymns, the hero is presented as a larger-than-life figure. Their accomplishments are praised publicly and all their activities are full of strength and courage. In Proverbs 31, the woman of noble character is a person of action. She is diligent, not shirking any responsibility. Her wise business decisions and vigorous work bring her household peace and security. Her husband and children publicly praise her and call her blessed. But unlike ancient military hymns, the Proverbs 31 woman is not conquering enemy kings or slaying wild beasts. She is praised for her wise, godly living that brings blessings to all those around her.

It's important to keep in mind that this poem is primarily a celebratory Bible passage. Though it contains principles to be gleaned, it's not a checklist for living up to some acceptable standard. It's a celebration of those who take the wisdom of Proverbs to heart. It's a vision of who we are and who we can become when we honor the Lord in all we do (Prov. 31:30).

Ruth, the Valiant Woman

In the Hebrew Bible, immediately following the book of Proverbs is the book of Ruth. The story of Ruth is about a non-Israelite widow who leaves the safety of her homeland to support her widowed mother-in-law and join the people of God in Israel. By the end of the story, Ruth marries a man of good character, has a newborn son, and the family's land is redeemed, thereby restoring Ruth's mother-in-law as well.

Midway through the story—while she is still an unmarried foreigner gleaning leftover grain in the fields, a most vulnerable position in society—Ruth is recognized as *esheth hayil*, a "woman of noble character" (Ruth 3:11). *Esheth hayil* is the same phrase used in Proverbs 31:10. The meaning of this Hebrew phrase is difficult to capture in only one way. See how these various English Bibles have translated it in Proverbs 31:

- "excellent wife" (ESV)

- "wife of noble character" (NIV)

- "virtuous and capable wife" (NLT)

- "valiant woman" (DRA)

- "virtuous woman" (KJV)

- "truly good wife" (CEV)

- "wife with strong character" (GW)

Proverbs 31 was meant to be read in context of the book of Proverbs, and more broadly the rest of Scripture as well. So what does the Proverbs 31 woman, the *esheth hayil*, look like—that person of noble, wise, strong, excellent, valiant character? She looks like Ruth.

Integrity, One Piece at a Time

Proverbs 10:9 says, "Whoever walks in integrity walks securely." What does it mean to have integrity? One way to think of it is in terms of a building. When a building is said to have structural integrity, it means that it can bear up under the load. It doesn't collapse from its own weight or the weight of what it is meant to carry. Constructing a building with structural integrity takes careful planning, a good deal of time, hard work from many people, and, of course, lots of patience when some things don't go as planned.

Integrity in our lives takes these things too. Consider what Paul lists in the New Testament as the qualities of a person who walks by the Holy Spirit: "The fruit of the Spirit is love, joy, peace, forbearance [or patience], kindness, goodness, faithfulness, gentleness and self-control" (Gal. 5:22–23). Sounds a lot like the traits we've been reading about in Proverbs, doesn't it?

None of these qualities happen overnight, and certainly not through our own effort alone. When we put our faith in Jesus as our Savior, his Holy Spirit resides within us to guide and empower us (see John 14). In this sense, the Spirit grows—or *builds*—these fruits in our lives. Like a structure being built with integrity, character comes through reliance on the Spirit in both painful times and joyous times; through failures and Plan B's; over stretches of time and with diligent work. As Paul also says, "We know that suffering produces perseverance; perseverance, character; and character, hope" (Rom. 5:3–4).

Live It

Wisdom Is for Passing On

King Lemuel had a wise mom; so wise, in fact, that her words of wisdom were placed in Scripture to be read by generations to come—including us right now (Prov. 31:1). Wisdom is for passing on to others. As the introduction to the book of Proverbs says, "These proverbs will give insight to the simple, knowledge and discernment to the young" (Prov. 1:4 NLT).

Guiding others in godly wisdom can take many forms. We might call it mentoring, discipling, teaching, or simply sharing your life with and loving those around you. No one needs to be super smart or all-knowing to do this. No one has to be as wise as Solomon or the heroic woman of Proverbs 31. But we do need to be people who "fear the LORD," because that's where real wisdom begins (Prov. 9:10). And it certainly helps to have a teachable heart (all the best teachers have one): "Apply your heart to instruction and your ears to words of knowledge" (Prov. 23:12).

The greatest teacher in the Bible said, "Take my yoke upon you and learn from me" (Matt. 11:29). Day by day as you learn from the Lord, grow in wisdom from his Word, and love those around you, you might just find that you've become someone else's ordinary hero too.

> ## "Speaking to five thousand people is no more important than quietly teaching one."
>
> —Tony Dungy

Life Application Questions

1. Who is someone you know personally who you'd say has integrity and character—an ordinary hero? What qualities about them do you admire?

2. What are some ways the Holy Spirit develops the character traits of the "fruit of the Spirit" in our lives?

3. Read Proverbs 16:32. Patience and self-control are both listed as fruits of the Spirit in Galatians 5:22–23. In what areas of your life could you use more patience and self-control?

4. Have you ever mentored or discipled someone? Have you had a mentor or discipleship leader yourself? What did you learn from those experiences?

5. What are some ways you could be more intentional about sharing godly wisdom with the people in your life?

6. Take some time to think back over the things discussed in this study on Proverbs. What is one area of your life you want focus on and grow more in godly wisdom? Write out a prayer for the Holy Spirit to work in and strengthen that part of your life.

Notes

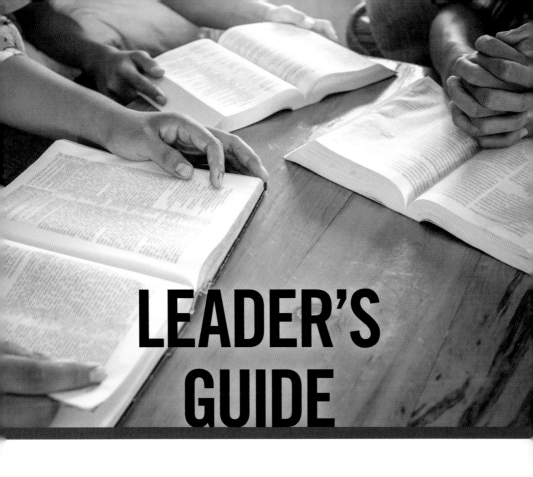

LEADER'S GUIDE

"Encourage one another and build each other up."

1 THESSALONIANS 5:11

Leader's Guide

Congratulations! You've either decided to lead a Bible study, or you're thinking hard about it. Guess what? God does big things through small groups. When his people gather together, open his Word, and invite his Spirit to work, their lives are changed!

Do you feel intimidated yet?

Be comforted by this: even the great apostle Paul felt "in over his head" at times. When he went to Corinth to help people grasp God's truth, he admitted he was overwhelmed: "I came to you in weakness with great fear and trembling" (1 Corinthians 2:3). Later he wondered, "Who is adequate for such a task as this?" (2 Corinthians 2:16 NLT).

Feelings of inadequacy are normal; every leader has them. What's more, they're actually healthy. They keep us dependent on the Lord. It is in our times of greatest weakness that God works most powerfully. The Lord assured Paul, "My grace is sufficient for you, for my power is made perfect in weakness" (2 Corinthians 12:9).

The Goal

What is the goal of a Bible study group? Listen as the apostle Paul speaks to Christians:

- "Oh, my dear children! I feel as if I'm going through labor pains for you again, and they will continue until *Christ is fully developed in your lives*" (Galatians 4:19 NLT, emphasis added).

- "For God knew his people in advance, and he chose them *to become like his Son*" (Romans 8:29 NLT, emphasis added).

Do you see it? God's ultimate goal for us is that we would become like Jesus Christ. This means a Bible study is not about filling our heads with more information. Rather, it is about undergoing transformation. We study and apply God's truth so that it will reshape our hearts and minds, and so that over time, we will become more and more like Jesus.

Paul said, "The purpose of my instruction is that all believers would be filled with love that comes from a pure heart, a clear conscience, and genuine faith" (1 Timothy 1:5 NLT).

This isn't about trying to "master the Bible." No, we're praying that God's Word will master us, and through humble submission to its authority, we'll be changed from the inside out.

Your Role

Many group leaders experience frustration because they confuse their role with God's role. Here's the truth: God alone knows our deep hang-ups and hurts. Only he can save a soul, heal a heart, fix a life. It is God who rescues people from depression, addictions, bitterness, guilt, and shame. We Bible study leaders need to realize that *we can't do any of those things.*

So what can we do? More than we think!

- We can pray.

- We can trust God to work powerfully.

- We can obey the Spirit's promptings.

- We can prepare for group gatherings.

- We can keep showing up faithfully.

With group members:

- We can invite, remind, encourage, and love.

- We can ask good questions and then listen attentively.

- We can gently speak tough truths.

- We can celebrate with those who are happy and weep with those who are sad.

- We can call and text and let them know we've got their back.

But we can never do the things that only the Almighty can do.

- We can't play the Holy Spirit in another person's life.

- We can't be in charge of outcomes.

- We can't force God to work according to our timetables.

And one more important reminder: besides God's role and our role, group members also have a key role to play in this process. If they don't show up, prepare, or open their hearts to God's transforming truth, no life change will take place. We're not called to manipulate or shame, pressure or arm twist. We're not to blame if members don't make progress—and we don't get the credit when they do. We're mere instruments in the hands of God.

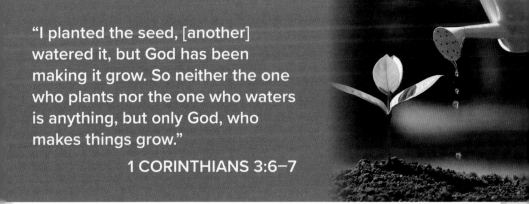

"I planted the seed, [another] watered it, but God has been making it grow. So neither the one who plants nor the one who waters is anything, but only God, who makes things grow."

1 CORINTHIANS 3:6–7

Leader Myths and Truths

Many people assume that a Bible study leader should:

- Be a Bible scholar.

- Be a dynamic communicator.

- Have a big, fancy house to meet in.

- Have it all together—no doubts, bad habits, or struggles.

These are myths—even outright lies of the enemy!

Here's the truth:

- God is looking for humble Bible students, not scholars.

- You're not signing up to give lectures, you're agreeing to facilitate discussions.

- You don't need a palace, just a place where you can have uninterrupted discussions. (Perhaps one of your group members will agree to host your study.)

- Nobody has it all together. We are all in process. We are all seeking to work out "our salvation with fear and trembling" (Philippians 2:12).

As long as your desire is that Jesus be Lord of your life, God will use you!

- You want to wow others with your biblical knowledge.

  "Love . . . does not boast, it is not proud"
  (1 Corinthians 13:4).

- You're seeking a hidden personal gain or profit.

  "We do not peddle the word of God for profit"
  (2 Corinthians 2:17).

- You want to tell people how wrong they are.

  "Do not condemn" (Romans 2:1).

- You want to fix or rescue people.

  "It is God who works in you to will and to act"
  (Philippians 2:13).

- You're being pressured to do it.

  "Am I now trying to win the approval of
  human beings, or of God?" (Galatians 1:10).

A Few Do's

✔ Pray for your group.

Are you praying for your group members regularly? It is the most important thing a leader can do for his or her group.

✔ Ask for help.

If you're new at leading, spend time with an experienced group leader and pick his or her brain.

✔ Encourage members to prepare.

Challenge participants to read the Bible passages and the material in their study guides, and to answer and reflect on the study questions during the week prior to meeting.

✔ Discuss the group guidelines.

Go over important guidelines with your group at the first session, and again as needed if new members join the group in later sessions. See the *Group Guidelines* at the end of this leader's guide.

✔ Share the load.

Don't be a one-person show. Ask for volunteers. Let group members host the meeting, arrange for snacks, plan socials, lead group prayer times, and so forth. The old saying is true: Participants become boosters; spectators become critics.

✔ Be flexible.

If a group member shows up in crisis, it is okay to stop and take time to surround the hurting brother or sister with love. Provide a safe place for sharing. Listen and pray for his or her needs.

✔ Be kind.

Remember, there's a story—often a heart-breaking one—behind every face. This doesn't *excuse* bad or disruptive behavior on the part of group members, but it might *explain* it.

A Few Don'ts

✘ Don't "wing it."

Although these sessions are designed to require minimum preparation, read each one ahead of time. Highlight the questions you feel are especially important for your group to spend time on.

✘ Don't feel ashamed to say, "I don't know."

Disciple means "learner," not "know-it-all."

✘ Don't feel the need to "dump the truck."

You don't have to say everything you know. There is always next week. A little silence during group discussion time, that's fine. Let members wrestle with questions.

✘ Don't put members on the spot.

Invite others to share and pray, but don't pressure them. Give everyone an opportunity to participate. People will open up on their own time as they learn to trust the group.

✘ Don't go down "rabbit trails."

Be careful not to let one person dominate the time or for the discussion to go down the gossip road. At the same time, don't short-circuit those occasions when the Holy Spirit is working in your group members' lives and therefore they *need* to share a lot.

✘ Don't feel pressure to cover every question.

Better to have a robust discussion of four questions than a superficial conversation of ten.

✘ Don't go long.

Encourage good discussion, but don't be afraid to "rope 'em back in" when needed. Start and end on time. If you do this from the beginning, you'll avoid the tendency of group members to arrive later and later as the season goes on.

How to Use This Study Guide

Many group members have busy lives—dealing with long work hours, childcare, and a host of other obligations. These sessions are designed to be as simple and straightforward as possible to fit into a busy schedule. Nevertheless, encourage group members to set aside some time during the week (even if it's only a little) to pray, read the key Bible passage, and respond to questions in this study guide. This will make the group discussion and experience much more rewarding for everyone.

Each session contains four parts.

Read It

The *Key Bible Passage* is the portion of Scripture everyone should read during the week before the group meeting. The group can read it together at the beginning of the session as well.

The *Optional Reading* is for those who want to dig deeper and read lengthier Bible passages on their own during the week.

Know It

This section encourages participants to reflect on the Bible passage they've just read. Here, the goal is to interact with the biblical text and grasp what it says. (We'll get into practical application later.)

Explore It

Here group members can find background information with charts and visuals to help them understand the Bible passage and the topic more deeply. They'll move beyond the text itself and see how it connects to other parts of Scripture and the historical and cultural context.

Live It

Finally, participants will examine how God's Word connects to their lives. There are application questions for group discussion or personal reflection, practical ideas to apply what they've learned from God's Word, and a closing thought and/or prayer. (Remember, you don't have to cover all the questions or everything in this section during group time. Focus on what's most important for your group.)

Celebrate!

Here's an idea: Have a plan for celebrating your time together after the last session of this Bible study. Do something special after your gathering time, or plan a separate celebration for another time and place. Maybe someone in your group has the gift of hospitality—let them use their gifting and organize the celebration.

	30-MINUTE SESSION	60-MINUTE SESSION
READ IT	Open in prayer and read the *Key Bible Passage.* 5 minutes	Open in prayer and read the *Key Bible Passage.* 5 minutes
KNOW IT	Ask: "What stood out to you from this Bible passage?" 5 minutes	Ask: "What stood out to you from this Bible passage?" 5 minutes
EXPLORE IT	Encourage group members to read this section on their own, but don't spend group time on it. Move on to the life application questions.	Ask: "What did you find new or helpful in the *Explore It* section? What do you still have questions about?" 10 minutes
LIVE IT	Members voluntarily share their answers to 3 or 4 of the life application questions. 15 minutes	Members voluntarily share their answers to the life application questions. 25 minutes
PRAYER & CLOSING	Conclude with a brief prayer. 5 minutes	Share prayer requests and praise reports. Encourage the group to pray for each other in the coming week. Conclude with a brief prayer. 15 minutes

90-MINUTE SESSION

Open in prayer and read the *Key Bible Passage.*

5 minutes

- Ask: "What stood out to you from this Bible passage?"
- Then go over the *Know It* questions as a group.

10 minutes

- Ask: "What did you find new or helpful in the *Explore It* section? What do you still have questions about?"
- Here, the leader can add information found while preparing for the session.
- If there are questions or a worksheet in this section, go over those as a group.

20 minutes

- Members voluntarily share their answers to the life application questions.
- Wrap up this time with a closing thought or suggestions for how to put into practice in the coming week what was just learned from God's Word.

30 minutes

- Share prayer requests and praise reports.
- Members voluntarily pray during group time about the requests and praises shared.
- Encourage the group to pray for each other in the coming week.

25 minutes

Group Guidelines

This group is about discovering God's truth, supporting each other, and finding growth in our new life in Christ. To reach these goals, a group needs a few simple guidelines that everyone should follow for the group to stay healthy and for trust to develop.

1. **Everyone agrees to make group time a priority.**
   We understand that there are work, health, and family issues that come up. So if there is an emergency or schedule conflict that cannot be avoided, be sure to let someone know that you can't make it that week. This may seem like a small thing, but it makes a big difference to your other group members.

2. **What is said in the group stays in the group.**
   Accept it now: we are going to share some personal things. Therefore, the group must be a safe and confidential place to share.

3. **Don't be judgmental, even if you strongly disagree.**
   Listen first, and contribute your perspective only as needed. Remember, you don't fully know someone else's story. Take this advice from James: "Be quick to listen, slow to speak, and slow to become angry" (James 1:19).

4. **Be patient with one another.**
   We are all in process, and some of us are hurting and struggling more than others. Don't expect bad habits or attitudes to disappear overnight.

5. **Everyone participates.**
   It may take time to learn how to share, but as you develop a trust toward the other group members, take the chance.

If you struggle in any of these areas, ask God's help for growth, and ask the group to help hold you accountable. Remember, you're all growing together.

Notes

ROSE VISUAL BIBLE STUDIES
6-Session Study Guides for Personal or Group Use

 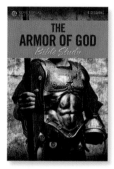 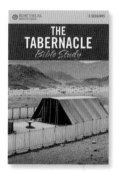 

THE BOOK OF JAMES
Find out what James says about cultivating a genuine living faith through six tests of faith.

THE ARMOR OF GOD
Dig deep into Ephesians 6 and learn the meaning of each piece of the armor.

THE TABERNACLE
Discover how each item of the tabernacle foreshadowed Jesus and what that means for us today.

THE LIFE OF PAUL
See how the apostle Paul persevered through trials and proclaimed the gospel.

 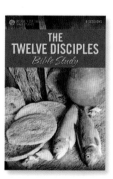 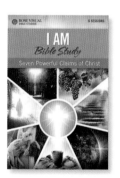 

JOURNEY TO THE RESURRECTION
Renew your heart and mind as you engage in spiritual practices. Perfect for Easter.

THE TWELVE DISCIPLES
Learn about the twelve men Jesus chose to be his disciples.

I AM
Know the seven powerful claims of Christ from the gospel of John.

PROVERBS
Gain practical, godly wisdom from the book of Proverbs.

www.hendricksonrose.com